# How to Make Money Everyday Blogging:
# For Full-Time Income

## Alicia Washington

# Table of Contents

# Introduction

My name is Alicia Washington and I am a full time blogger and owner of Workersonboard.com – a legitimate database of work at home jobs that are posted several times a week with real companies that hire people to work from home.

My personal journey into blogging really began when I first learned of a few companies that would pay you to write articles from home.  I came discover that I actually enjoyed sharing information to others, especially if it was helpful.  One day, I came across a blog post where someone wrote an article about their own experiences blogging for themselves and I thought to give it a try.

At this time, I didn't have any experience or knowledge about how to do this, what was needed, any technical skills and so forth.  I only knew how to browse the Internet and how to write an article.  Little did I know, that writing articles and publishing them online was all I needed to know and I could learn the rest later.  I had the basics down.  Come up with a title, elaborate on it in the post and publish it.  If I could do this, then I could start my own blog.

I was nervous but determined to make it work.  I read and researched on blogging as much as I could along with hands on experience and I am so glad that I decided to give it a try.

My purpose of writing this book is to encourage you to do the same.  Do not let anyone tell you that you cannot do this because I am proof that it is possible to start and maintain a successful blog with little to no experience at all.

To date, my main blog is around 3 years old and I couldn't have written this book back then and that is why I have decided to do it now to share with you my personal experiences blogging and how it has helped me to earn a full time income from home.

As a matter of fact, anybody can do this no matter where you live or what age you are.  Whether you live in Russia, have 8 kids at home, work a couple of jobs outside the home, you can start a blog on your own terms.  Setting your own schedule,  writing whenever you want and earning money all at the same time.  This book is designed to share with you all the techniques that I have used that have really worked for me that you can also incorporate into your blog to help you to reach your goals.

If you would like to see this information presented in video form, please go to my active YouTube channel and search for the name Super2Moms or Workersonboard and you will find videos tutorials about how to put ads on a blog, how to write an article and so much more!

Please do not be intimidated about the idea of blogging.  This book is an easy read with terms and illustrations that you can relate to.  It is simple, practical and realistic so that you can get started blogging right after you finish this book.

I hope that you enjoy this book and share it with your family, friends, co-workers, acquaintances and others to give them a boost and other options that they can pursue right from their computer.

# What is a blog?

A blog is basically a platform to express your thoughts, ideas, opinions, words, etc. Some have even referred to it as being an online diary.  Why? Because it can be compared to a journal where you keep a record of your thoughts on a regular basis. The only difference with a blog is that it is more of an open diary because you will now be sharing your knowledge and so forth on the world wide web.  When your posts are published live, it is now available for the entire world to see.

If you are a person that has ever had a journal, keeps a journal, or even likes the idea of doing this online, blogging will be very natural for you.  Even if you have never done any of these things before, blogging is something that anyone can do because everybody has either a story to tell, some tips to share, knows something that you don't know, or has the desire to help others.

## There are some misconceptions about blogging or having a blog.  Here are some of the more common ones

- You have to know something about computers to be able to blog.
- It will cost you money to get a blog.
- You must be an expert in order to blog.
- You have to know html, coding, CSS, etc. in order to be able to blog.
- You have to be a writer in order to blog.

I only listed a few, of course there are more misconceptions about having a blog or blogging in general but none of the ones I mentioned are true.  These are simply myths.  As I stated earlier, anyone can do this.  Whether you are a student, a teenager, mother, teacher, parent, retired, or whatever your status in life is, if you can type, you can blog.  How do I know this?  Because I got started blogging about 3 years ago with absolutely no knowledge whatsoever about blogging.  I am a stay at home mom with 3 children who are age 10 and under with a very demanding schedule.  The only thing that I knew how to do was to log on to my computer and search the Internet.  I didn't even know what a blog was.  Blogging was something that I never thought that I would do not because I didn't want to but because I didn't know how.

It is so much easier than I thought it would be.  I actually wished that I would have started blogging sooner.  You don't have to wait.  You can start your own free blog right now from Blogger.com Weebly or for less than $10 at GoDaddy!  You can also try Host Gator, Host Papa or Host Monster for hosting.  The possibilities and opportunities of what you can do with a blog are limitless.  You can build an online presence, brand yourself, and even have people follow you.  All the tools that you need to blog are right at your fingertips.  You may even come to feel that way that I do about blogging, that you wished you would have done this sooner.  This blog is dedicated to helping anyone get started blogging right from the very beginning.  Please join me on this journey so that we can learn, grow, and have fun together blogging.

# How to Write a Blog Post

For those who are new at blogging, creating your first post may be quite challenging especially if you don't know exactly how to tackle this or what angle to go about creating a post. If you are spontaneous and you tend to write that way, your thoughts or post could start out a certain way and end up going completely in another direction altogether than what you originally intended. If you stick to the topic or can relate back to the main point, this may not necessarily be a bad thing. But if it veers completely off course, your post may lose steam and your audience could quickly become sidetracked.

There are a few techniques that you can utilize and incorporate into your posts that will help you engage your audience. Some can be in the form of a question and answer post, how to solve a problem, a review, a numbered listing of tips, ideas, advice, etc. You could also create a post on a very controversial subject or topic in the form of a statement or question like "**10 Reasons Why Tiger Woods should never remarry**".

After you have created or come up with a title for your post, you will want to start off with an introduction of at least 3 sentences. Your introduction can contain more than 3 sentences but make sure that it is not too long because your introduction really should serve the purpose of grabbing your readers attention. In your introduction tell the reader what they can expect in the post, what it will accomplish, and how it can benefit them. Not necessarily in this order, but you get the idea.

The body of the post is the heart of the article where it actually breaks down the steps of what you want your reader to learn, gain, or know.  It should be practical and easy to follow so that the reader will not get overwhelmed.  You can use the body of the post to relate to your reader and have a connection with them by including a personal experience, having empathy and sensitivity for your readers, and most importantly how the information can enrich their lives in some form or fashion.

The summary is where you will include the main points of your posts concisely.  It has been said, that people generally remember the last thing they hear so you can make good use of your summary to encourage your readers to put into action what they just read.  It is also beneficial to include a positive thought at this time so that your readers will be built up by what you just wrote.  Here is a sample blog post idea that could help you to accomplish this.

**Blog Post Example**

**Can I Make a Full Time Living Blogging Online?**  (Sample Title)

You have seen and read where bloggers have the potential to make a full time living writing online.  Could this just be another scam?  How can the average person do this?  What kind of skills will I need?  Blogging might be easier than what you may think and this post will explain how you can do this, how to get started, as well as how much you can make blogging in your spare time. (Sample Introduction)

From here the post will practically write itself on the body.

Now that you know that you really can make a full time living blogging online, what is stopping you from doing this? Nothing has to. You can start right now today, blogging your way to achieve your goal of being able to earn a full time living right from your computer. (Sample summary/ending)

# 20 Reasons to Start a Blog

There are many reasons that people start writing blogs. The most basic of reasons is to share what you do in your life with family and friends. It's exciting when new people subscribe to your blog to be able to read about your day to day life or what you're accomplishing with your diet, business or parenting skills. Another reason to start a blog is to make money.  Making money with a blog is not only exciting, but absolutely financially rewarding as well.  When deciding on whether you should professionally blog to earn money you have a couple of choices to make. You can start your own blog and write about the things in life that you have a passion for, or you can find a company that needs bloggers to write freelance work for them or actually be on their employee payroll.

Starting your own personal blog will take time to build an audience and actually start earning so be prepared to continue working a real paying job when you're starting up. You may be asking why you should start a blog?  How will it really benefit you and how can you get started?  I have complied a short list to answer some of the questions you may have.

## 1. Your Life Will have Purpose

You heard that right! Once you begin to blog on a daily basis you will begin to see the things about your life that you want to really focus on.

You'll have a chance to really begin to see which direction your life is going, who you really are and what you truly want to do in your life. Aside from making money, being able to direct your life on a route to gain more success and achieve the most is definitely a positive thing to have. Gaining purpose in life as each new day arrives.

## 2.   Meeting new and exciting people

When you start blogging be prepared for an influx of new people coming into your life. Besides just having a few comments on your blog posts or people clicking "like" on what you have written, you will potentially be forming relationships with new friends from around the globe. When you blog, you'll be amazed at how people want to see you do well with your blog.

## 3. You will be an Inspiration to others

Did you think blogging was all about you? Well think again! When you start a blog, you start to be an inspiration to all of those who subscribe to your blog. People from around the world will seemingly tune in daily to catch a glimpse of your life and thoughts and feelings. You are going to inspire people! Your blog gives them a reason to turn their computer on each day. Yes it will take time to build your audience but once you do, you'll find that you're touching lives in ways you never thought possible. As an old saying goes "It only take a spark to start a fire." Be that spark and start a flame that wraps around the world and around the people who are reading your blog!

## 4. It's not going to cost you anything!

Blogging is something that anyone who knows how to turn on a computer and sign up on a free website can do. It will never cost you even one penny to start a blog. Using a site like Wordpress.com is always free, and is one of the most highly recommended sites to begin blogging. Sure, you can use a service to create your own personal domain name and those sites charge a small fee but overall blogging is not going to cost you anything.

## 5. Blogging can help you grow business to your established business!

If you have a small business already and have struggled to get it up and running, having a blog can definitely increase your income. Start blogging about the things your business does daily. Once you build your audience, you'll begin to see more business coming your way due to word of mouth. Keep your blog interesting and engaging so people will want to see what you're saying every day. People share what they like and when you have an interesting blog it is bound to be shared by people.

## 6. You'll gain confidence

Maybe you already consider yourself a confident person, but if you aren't always confident then starting a blog will put you on the right track to be able to build confidence.

Once you see how your audience is responding and growing your confidence is going to grow right along with them.

## 7. Your brain will grow stronger

When you start blogging you start thinking more.  When you think more, your brain develops more strongly.  Having a strong brain can help deter illnesses such as Alzheimer's and early onset dementia.  So use your brain and make it as strong as possible!

## 8. Blogging improves your writing skills

Maybe you have always wanted to write a book or would like to write articles for companies but never felt you had what it takes. When you begin blogging your writing skills begin to improve over time.  Daily blogging will increase your knowledge and you'll start writing better just from the day to day activities on your blog.

## 9.    You'll increase your popularity!

Blogging has become the most popular thing to do online for 20-35 year olds. When you create a new blog and stick to it you are bound to increase your overall popularity.

## 10. You will make money!

Reports have shown that 90% of businesses who have a daily blog have been able to pick up new customers due to their blogs alone.

## 11. People will trust you!

Up to 80% of all people who read blogs on a daily basis tend to trust the things they read in blogs.  When you blog, you have the opportunity to share your knowledge with the entire world!

## 12. You can keep track of your life as it develops

When you start a blog and keep it up daily you'll be able to look back on your life and see how you have grown, matured and developed.  You'll see the ways that you have changed your life and grown your blog to the point of making it work financially for you.

## 13. You will learn how to be a more committed person!

When you start a blog and you want to start earning a living from it you will finally learn what commitment is all about.  It takes time to start earning money from a blog and commitment is the key to making it work.  Success does not happen overnight so be prepared for possibly months before you can start making money but stick with it because in the long run anything is possible.

## 14.    You will never be unemployed!

While you may or may not have a full or part time job outside of your home, when you blog you will never be fully unemployed.  Put your writing skills to work for you and start earning some money by blogging!

## 15. You can be the cure to a lonely heart!

Many people who sit and read blogs have no social life outside of their homes. They have no one they can talk to or rely on.  When you stay consistent with your blog, you are in essence, the one friend that some people may have.  They begin to rely on you and your words of wisdom or your humor or advice.  You and you alone can be the cure they need for their loneliness.  The more lonely hearts who start following you, the better chance you have of making money.

## 16. You're the boss!!

When you start blogging to earn a living you have suddenly walked away from the stress of working for someone else and have become your own boss.  While it may be stressful to worry about earning a living from blogging, your creative side will take over and you'll find yourself more committed to making a blog work when you know you can actually pay your bills from it.

## 17. You suddenly become the shopping guru!

More than 70% of consumers say they have purchased something based on what a person's individual blog has recommended.  If you place links on your blog for products you personally sue and enjoy, people are bound to trust your instincts and will buy them as well.  If you're recommending products, you could pick up companies who ask you to advertise their products on your blog so they can sell them.  This is definitely going to make you some well-earned money.

## 18. You ego will be boosted!

When you run a blog you are going to have so many new people liking what you have to say. Strangers will start commenting on how they love what you wrote or how they agree with your opinions. These things will give your ego an incredible boost upwards!

## 19. You will be able to form relationships with businesses

When you blog for money, you're not going to make money on just the blog alone. While your writing skills may be impeccable you're still going to need businesses to advertise or who will want you to sell their products from your blog site. Once you gain enough followers businesses will seek you out to sell or advertise for them. These are your money makers!

## 20. You will be searchable!!!

When you start a blog you are suddenly entered into the search engines on Google and Bing. The more traffic your blog has, the higher you will be listed when people search. Being listed on Google or Bing is definitely going to bring more traffic to your page and will eventually start you on the road to earning a living from blogging!

# How to Get People to Read your Blog

You are excited about the latest blog post you have just created. You put a lot of time, energy, and hard work into creating good, quality content for your visitors. As a matter of fact, it may be one of your best posts to date, but what if no one is reading it? If this is happening or has happened to you there may be a simple solution to your problem.  What is it?  I will explain what you can do in 10 easy steps to get people to read your blog.

First let me start by saying that it can be a very frustrating and disappointing thing to have a blog that you are proud of and have no one read it.  It can be compared to throwing papers in the wind.  Those papers may contain beautiful poetry, staff or musical notes, or even creative artwork.  Of course they have value but it remains to be unseen because no one has taken the time to look at it or in your case read it.

Some people say that you need a built in audience to get others to read your blog but your content can actually draw in an audience.  Especially is this the case if you write a particular post and it goes viral or is spread around to several people online.  But how can you get that first person to read it?  Here are a few tips that can help you to accomplish this.

1.  **Killer Titles** - A lot of times people will overlook a post if the title does not capture their attention.  Magazines are very good at using catchy titles to get your attention.  You have probably noticed while you are waiting in line to check

out of the grocery store a phrase or title from a magazine intrigues you to pick it up and read it.  You can use this technique also when you are creating a blog post.  For example, say you are going to write an article about how to decorate your house on a budget.  Instead of saying that you try this, **"How to decorate your home for less than $50"**.

**2.  Give Details** - This kind of goes along with what I just mentioned in the first tip.  When you give details in your title, it will give your visitors something to look forward to and will encourage them to read your post.  You only have a few seconds to capture their attention and that is why the title is very important.  An example, instead of saying, "How to make a meal in 30 minutes", which is good but "How to Make 5 Delicious Home Cooked Meals in less than 30 minutes" is even better.  Try not to give too many details but just enough to spark their interest.

3.  **Controversy** - I once asked this same question myself about how to get people to read your blog and one of the responses that I was given was to talk about a controversial topic.  Why?  Because it is very effective.  Whatever niche your blog or website is related around you can come up with a controversial topic to stir up interest in your posts.  I once wrote an article entitled, **"Why I stopped writing for Hubpages"** on my other blog and it got people to read it and start conversations about this subject.  Give it a try and you will see some results.

**4. Rumors** - Rumors and controversy go hand in hand as well.  If you notice, a lot of talk show personalities, celebrities, media and entertainment companies employ this technique to keep their audience in suspense or to steal away their competitions audience.  If there is a rumor going around use it to your advantage and explore this topic.  Don't be afraid to discuss it in your posts.  For example, maybe you have heard that Apple is losing steam in the tech world, you could talk about that or maybe you have heard that a certain company has decreased the pay of their employees or independent contractors who work for them. Anything like this could help you to get people to read your blog.

**5. Make your posts relatable** - Talk about things that the average person or even your next door neighbor could relate to. You don't have to use fancy wording or even be perfect in your grammar but you do want your posts to speak to your audience. Have them in mind when you are creating content for your blog or website.

**6. Be Realistic** - If you have a blog about how to make money online, it would be much better to tell them how they could earn $20 a day using social media rather than stating that they could earn $7,000 a month from their computer when they are just learning how to do this. It may be enticing to attract them with large figures but try to resist this approach because it could backfire. You don't want to exaggerate or leave them with such high hopes that they get discouraged if they don't achieve it. You may get some of the blame and you don't want to have a reputation of being an exaggerator. Start off with something more attainable and gradually open them up to more ideas and other ways that they can earn more money.

**7. Informative** - Try to give as much information as possible. Maybe you are writing a post about how to make a homemade apple pie. Lay out all the steps for them and include photos or videos as well. If you don't provide it for them they may decide to find it somewhere else. This may include but not limited to some tips, charts, examples, short cut techniques and the like because everybody is always on the lookout for simpler, easier ways to get things done.

**8. Have your audience in mind** - Think about things that interest them and talk about that. In order to do this, you almost have to put yourself in their situation. Lets say you have a parenting blog where you could discuss several topics geared toward parents. You could talk about the advantages of home schooling, preparing healthy meals for the family, taking vacations, and all kinds of things.  Sharing your family photos and vacation pictures may not be the best method unless they will benefit from it and you focus your attention back on the reader.  If you want to show them how to have the kids help you bake a cake and you add photos of everyone participating in the activity and the finished product, this would be appropriate.  Your blog should be about them and not yourself unless this was your intention in the very beginning.  Famous and well-known personalities can get away with this because people are curious and interested in them.

**9.**  They will even search the Internet to find out more information about them on a regular basis.  It is much better to stick to things they will really appreciate and benefit from unless of course, your audience wants to know more about you and you are asked to share your personal experiences and so forth.  The decision to do so is up to your own personal discretion.

**10.  Start Discussions** - If you are part of a forum or online community, start a question or answer one using your own post to get others to read it.  This can prove to be especially effective if that community is related to your blog post or topic.  The audience is already there, you just have to navigate or redirect them to your blog.  For example, say you have joined a tech community and you have written a great post about some cool smartphone apps.  Start a discussion on this topic or answer a question someone has asked about some smartphone apps and leave a link to your blog post or include it in your signature.  Just make sure you don't spam.  If you haven't joined an online community, you may want to do this as soon as you can if you want your posts to be read.

**11.  Share** - How many times have we heard this.  Several, but it is true that if you share your posts there is a greater chance that they will get read. Share them everywhere you can.  On Facebook, Twitter, Pinterest, Stumbled Upon, Reddit, and anywhere else you can think of.  Every time you write a post, share it.  Don't underestimate the power of Social Media and use it as a vehicle to get people to read your blog.


Now these are not hard and fast rules just a few tips that could help your posts get read.  We know how important readers are to a blog.  Without it, it is like papers in the wind.  What techniques will you use to get people to read your blog?

# How to set up a Wordpress Blog

There are many reasons in which you would want to set up a blog for yourself or for a business. It can be an outlet for you to let your individual voice be heard, to share your knowledge, or to promote a service or product.  No matter what the reason may be, setting up a blog on Wordpress is very easy to use to do and can be accomplished in just a few simple steps.  Here is exactly how you would do it.

Your first step would be to go to Wordpress.com or Wordpress.org in your address bar. This will bring you to their site where you then will go to the left side of the page and click on the get started button. This will bring you to a page where you would then enter all of your information and the way in which you would be using the blog. Wordpress blogs are not only easy to use but they are free.

Once you have entered all of your information you are able to see all of the design styles in which you would be able to use. These are all beautiful but can be chosen based on someones particular style.  You are also able to personalize it more by making your own web address to use behind the Wordpress site. Which is all right on the page which it prompts you with.

Maintaining your blog is also very easy and can be done by looking at the left side bar and seeing all of options in which you have to enhance your site. Some of the options allow you to change the colors and the titles of your pages.

If you are looking to enhance your blog site even further you are able to buy more advancements in Wordpress. The basic package which is free allows you to change the appearance and the content which goes on your blog as much and as extensive as you would like.

The process in which you endure going into it goes through a few steps, you register, you chose your domain name which you would like to be after the Wordpress site, you are brought to a page where you decide your theme and color scheme and then you are complete in the set up process for your blogging site.

The next step is to have your pages be exactly what you would like them to display to those visiting your site. This can be changed under the pages section, once there you are able to click on a page you would like and it will bring you to the page where you can change the name of your page and update it.

If you acquire a Wordpress.org blog, make sure that you purchase hosting on sites like Host Gator, Go Daddy, Host Papa, Host Monster, Web Hosting Pad, My Hosting, Just Host and others for as low as $1.99 per month and up.

You can express so much through a blog so why not use the easiest system around?

# How to Make Money using Google Adsense

You have probably heard or know someone who is earning money from Google Adsense. But is this really a legitimate way to earn money from your blog and if so, how can this be accomplished? I will explain in this post how anyone can earn money from Google Adsense and exactly what you can do to increase your earnings also.

In order to make money from Google Adsense you will need online content. This could be in the form of a blog or website or on video. Many people generally start using Google Adsense on their blog/website. It only takes a few minutes to sign up for a free account. Before you do so, make sure that you have enough content on your blog, roughly 10 pages or so with original, quality content. This will ensure that your account will be approved without any delays in just a few short days. After you have been approved, you will go to your Google Adsense publisher account and get the codes to place on your blog.

Where you place your ads will affect how much you can earn from Google Adsense. If you place your ads too far down the page, your visitors may miss or overlook them. When this happens, you are less likely to get clicks.  It is much better to place your ads towards the top of the page so your visitors will see them.  Another technique is to put your ads right among the content where your visitors will be reading.  You can also place your ads randomly from the halfway point of the page and upwards from there so they will be visible to everyone.

You can maximize your clicks by testing out different size ads to see which are more effective.  Wider size ads tend to perform better than the smaller ads.  Here are some of the sizes that Google recommends for the most exposure.

- 300 x 250 medium rectangle
- 336 x 280 large rectangle
- 728 x 90 horizontal leaderboard
- 160 x 600 wide skyscraper
- 320 x 50 mobile banner

You have the option of picking other sizes but when you are first starting out with Google Adsense, it is better to choose the recommended ads to maximize your visibility, engagement, and income potential.  After the ads have been placed, you really don't have to do anything else but continue to publish content on a regular basis.  To keep your site from looking cluttered, you are only allowed 3 Google ad units per page.

Putting ads on your blog is the easy part.  Now you have to get your blog noticed, read, or discovered.  Even if you have mastered the art of ad placement, without an audience, your blog will seem to disappear and fall under the radar.  This is exactly what you don't want.  When this happens, your earnings will fail to reach or warrant the amount of time and energy that you have put into it.  What you really need is traffic, traffic, and more traffic.  With a steady stream of traffic to your site, your earnings will continue to increase over time.  But where do you find your audience?

They are there, you just have to guide them to you.  Here are some practical ways to reach your targeted audience.

- Article marketing
- Video marketing
- Commenting on related blogs
- Guest blogging
- Posting on forums
- Ebooks/books
- Social media
- Fiverr to promote your blog for $5

As you can see, it is very easy to make money with Google Adsense because it is passive income.  It may take a little time in the beginning, for you to reap the benefits of your content but continue to blog, write, and eventually you will earn money.  It could be even sooner than you think.

Since I wrote this post about Google Adsense, I though I would answer a question that I get asked a lot.  Can you post other affiliate ads along with Google Adsense?

Yes you can.  That is one of the things that I like about Google Adsense.  You can post other ad units from various affiliate companies in conjunction with theirs for greater earning potential.

# How to get traffic to your forum or blog

Have you just started a blog or forum and you have no blog comments or members registering to start and contribute to discussions on your online community?  Is your blog or forum fairly new and you would like to give it a jump start?  Or maybe you would just like to have more traffic to your site.  If you find yourself searching for ways to get more traffic to your blog or forum there may be an easy way for you to resolve this problem.  How?  By using a site called Postloop.

Postloop is an ingenious idea that helps blog and forum owners to get the traffic and content they desire.  Why is this so important?  A blog without comments or a forum community that is empty is likely to remain that way unless it becomes active.  It is very hard to get users to register to your forum or blog readers to comment on your blog if they feel that no one will read it or they will not be able to interact with others.  Blog commenters feed off of others comments and responses.  If there are no comments for them to read and look over, they may hesitate or bypass leaving a comment altogether.  Blog owners need, want and thrive off their blog readers opinions.  The more blog comments they get on their blog and posters they obtain for their forum will help to stimulate interest in their posts and ultimately will drive more traffic to their site.

It almost seemed to be impossible to overcome this challenge but Postloop has opened up the way for blog and forum owners to get the traffic they want and for content writers to earn extra money sharing relevant, valuable content on subjects and topics that interest them.  This is a win win situation for everyone.

If you own a blog or forum all you have to do is to submit your forum to Postloop, download the Postloop file or plugin for your blog and upload it to your forums directory and list all of your sites information.  It only takes 3 simple steps and your blog or forum will be available to the public and ready for blog comments or posts on your forum.  You will have to purchase points for a certain amount of dollars but you can also earn points rating your forum posters as well!

If you are struggling with content or traffic to your forum or blog, Postloop is a great solution to this problem. Remember membership is free and you always have the option to remove your forum or blog whenever you have garnered enough interest. Click here to try Postloop today and you will see an immediate difference in your traffic and content.

# How a Blog Makes Money?

Have you ever wondered how a blog makes money?  Could it be as simple as acquiring a blog and randomly placing ads in visible spots for others to see?  Yes and no.  The concept behind making money with a blog is through ad placement but it involves a little bit more than that.  As a matter of fact, there are a variety of ways that this can be accomplished.  Some techniques you may be familiar with and others not so much.  It really goes back to the advertisers.  They are the ones who set aside funds to promote their various products, businesses, services and so forth.  This topic will explain how a blog makes money and the variety of ways this can be achieved.

In order for you to make money with a blog, you must have one. You can get one for free or purchase one if you choose to do so. After you have your blog, you will want to come up with an topic or idea that your blog will be centered around.  There are no right or wrongs in this area because your blog is somewhat of a representation of you.  What your skills, knowledge, expertise or areas of interest.  If your blog has subjects that you enjoy talking about you will more likely create content for your readers on a regular basis.  This will benefit you in two ways.  First, your readers will keep coming back to your blog and they will most likely share your content with others.  Also, you will not get burned out so easily because you enjoy what you are sharing and look forward to creating posts for your audience.

Once you have your blog topic firmly in mind and a design that is appealing to you, you are ready to get started sharing content online.  After you have enough relevant content on your blog, you can sign up with several companies to be a publisher to promote and market well-known brands in the form of banner, text link, in-line text and other ads on your blog.  You earn a commission for each sale, click through, action or impression of the ads.  Make sure that your ads are visible and placed subsequently throughout your blog.  Most companies pay your commissions to you monthly either by check in the mail or through your Paypal account.  If you have not earned any commissions or failed to reach your payment threshold, your earnings will roll over until the next month.  Some companies that you can sign up with to be a publisher are:

**Panthera Network** (my personal favorite)
Google Adsense
Link Share
Chitika
Share a Sale
Commission Junction
Amazon
Ebay
Infolinks
Kontera

Reward it Media
Skimlinks
Media.net
Viglinks
and several others

It is free to sign up to be a publisher for these and other companies.  When you initially sign up, you may have to wait a couple of business days so that they can verify your blog stats, ranking, and other information for your publisher account to be approved.  After it is approved, you can select which advertisers you would like to promote based upon your blog's topics and categories.  For example, if you have a blog about shoes you will have more success promoting advertisers like Zappos, Shoe Dazzle, DSW, Macy's and other department stores.  This will help you to get better click through rates and generate sales for those advertisers.

There are other ways that you can earn money from a blog as well.  You can sell advertising spots on your blog and leave them open for individuals, companies, businesses and others to pay you to sponsor their company.  You can do this in the form of those square banner ads 125 x 125, 728 x 90 leaderboards or whatever method you feel is more beneficial for your blog and blog readers.  You can set a monthly price rate for the advertiser to purchase or negotiate a price they would be willing to pay.

Here are some additional ways you can make money with a blog.

Sponsored posts
Sponsored review
Selling your own products (ebooks, books, tshirts, etc.) highly recommend
As a consultant
Giving away free stuff
Referring others

This is the basics of how a blog makes money.  In order to make a monthly income from your blog, you will need an audience.  The best way to do this is to remain true to your blog's topics and not fabricate or copy any one else's content.  Be original and interact with your audience by allowing them to leave comments, share your posts, be able to contact you with questions or other concerns and most importantly write quality content on a regular basis.

# 5 Things Every Blogger Needs

If I would have known everything that I know now about blogging, my approach would have somewhat different.  For example, I didn't realize that blogging can be very demanding and challenging at times.  Not only do you have to make a weekly schedule that you will devote to making posts on your blog but you also need to think of new ideas and topics for your readers as well.  It takes a lot of planning and forethought. This is also true when you are in development of your own blog. That is why I wrote this post, to share with you 5 things that you need to know before you start your very own blog or website.

1.  **Dedication** - If you look this word up in the dictionary, it is defined as being dedicated or committed to a task or purpose.  This is absolutely essential when it comes to blogging.  Think of your blog as your business.  If you owned a coffee shop, would you show up for work that day and have no one cover for you or show up late in the day.  Of course not.  If you did, you would eventually lose customers and your business would not be received well and possibly incur a bad reputation.  No one wants that, especially when they are just starting out.  Look at your blog on a long term basis not just what rewards or benefits you will reap in the short term.  Think about the lasting effects your content will

have on your readers and how it can help them in their everyday lives.  By doing this, you will be compelled to do your best.  You will not leave your readers in the loop for weeks on end. You will be inspired to write posts in a timely fashion because you are dedicated to your blog.  Being dedicated to your blog means that you are dedicated to your readers as well.

**2.  Network** - Having a group of people that you connect with can help to boost your blog.  This is especially effective if they are in the same niche or area of interest that your blog is related around because they can help to promote your posts, share them in social media, and so forth.  This also helps to validate your blog.  If you don't have one already, you could find others in your niche and reach out to them, share their posts, guest blog for them, re tweet their messages, write quality content, and in time they may do the same for you.  A network is vital because it helps to build up a foundation for your blog which is important when you are just starting out.

**3.  Patience** - A lack of patience has led many bloggers to leave their blog idle, push it to the side, or abandon it entirely.  This does not have to happen to you.  Try not to expect immediate results.  For example, did you know that Subway restaurants began using this name back in 1968.  No one ever really heard of it until the mid 1980's or early 90's.  It didn't really become popular until the late 90's.  According to **Wikipedia**, "Subway is now the largest fast food chain in the world surpassing more restaurants than McDonald's."  Who would have ever thought that would happen?  That would not be the case if the owner(s) had given up on their idea.  The same is true about blogging.  It will take time, a lot of hard work, and consistent effort to reach it's full potential and carve out an audience for itself.  I am not implying that it will take 20+ years but the example I related just shows that patience will go a long way.

**4.  Thick Skin** - A blogger will need thick skin.  Every time you go to publish a post, your blog will be subject to criticism.  Everyone is a critic, including you.  If it is constructive criticism, welcome it and embrace it.  It is only going to help you to be a better blogger.  Sometimes the criticism may be harsh or unfair and that is exactly why I said that you will need thick skin. You would not believe how many times I have been told this won't work or your blog will never make it, and so forth but do not let that stop you. The only way you will know for sure is if you try it and see for yourself. Sculptors and artists use criticism to perfect their work, not define it and so can you.

**5.  Persistence** - Paparazzi are notorious for being persistent when they are in pursuit of getting a photo of a famous celebrity.  Those who are unemployed or out of work are also very persistent in looking for jobs on a regular basis. Bloggers also need to be persistent and have the same mentality when they encounter difficulties or obstacles to continue blogging.  There may be times when it will get easier and then not so much but if you are persistent with your blogging habits and efforts, your blog will be able to sustain these challenges including criticism that I mentioned earlier, competition, comparisons, and anything else I forgot to mention.


This topic was to enlighten and share with you some of the things that I have come to learn and experience as a blogger myself. Have you encountered any of these things yourself?

# 10 Must Haves for all Bloggers

When starting out with your own blog there are a few things that you must have that will help you increase your presence online. Why is this necessary? Because there is so much competition on the Internet today. Statistics show that there is a new blog born every second. More than half of the blogs created will be abandoned or even cease to exist altogether. Many times it is due to the fact that their blog is not generating the kind of traffic that the blogger intended to have so they may decide to give up blogging altogether.

That is exactly why I created this post, to share with you some of the things that I incorporate and use on my own blogs that have gotten results. Have I made mistakes and errors along the way? Absolutely, and I will probably continue to do so but you can learn from them and use it to your advantage. One of the things that I refrained from doing for a long time was to get on Facebook. I thought that it could not really benefit my blog because I looked at it as more of a social platform that would allow you to connect with your friends and family. But it is so much more than that. Facebook is an easy way for you make your blog official (so to speak). Your blog or your business, which your blog is your business is now on Facebook. You can interact with your readers, get feedback from them, and build up a following online. Had I got on Facebook sooner, I would have been able to reach more people. Do not underestimate the power of Facebook.

Facebook is just one thing that all bloggers must have.  I have a few more must have for those who are already blogging or thinking about getting their own blog that really works.  Here are some suggestions that you can try as well.

1.  **Social Media** - As I already mentioned social media is a must have for all bloggers because if your followers like what you share, they will in turn share it will others also, which will bring more traffic to your site.  Some of the more popular social media sites are:  Twitter, Facebook, Instagram, Pinterest, YouTube, and Tumblr just to name a few.

2.  **Statistics for your Blog** - Google Analytics or <u>Stat Counter</u> will do just fine.  They are both free services that will help you to see and analyze how many visitors you get to your site daily, what keywords they are using to find you, how long they stay on your site, what country they are from and so on.  This is important to know because you can use this data to leverage yourself when companies seek out your blog for advertising slots.  It will also be helpful to know how you audience found you and what they type in on the search engines to find you.  When you sign up to be a publisher for various affiliate companies, many times they will want to know your blog stats and Stat Counter will make it very easy you to do this.

3.  **Domain** - Having a subdomain for your blog is good but a domain is even better.  Instead of your blog saying Katie's Reviews.blogspot.com or wordpress.com it will not say Katie's Reviews.com.  This is not to say that your blog will not be successful with a subdomain but a domain gives you more control, can be easier to find, and is a lot cheaper than

you think.  I purchased mine domain for only $10 for the whole year from <u>Go Daddy</u>. Right now they have a special for .coms for just **$4**!

**4.  Follow Me Buttons** - Once you have signed up with your social media accounts, make sure that you have them visible on your blog.  It is better to have them closer to the top of your page so your visitors won't miss them. They can follow you with the touch of a mouse.  How easy is that! This way, they will never miss out on any posts, updates, or information you want to share with them.

**5.  RSS Feed** - Some websites may not necessarily come with rss feeds but many blogs do.  RSS or really simple syndication is a series of blog entries that your readers can look over without having to search through your blog for the latest information.  Having this tool makes it very convenient for your readers to get to your content quickly.

6.  <u>**Link Within**</u> - This is a must have for all bloggers, especially if you want to keep your readers on your blog longer.  Each time you create a new post, there will be 3 related posts in the form of a thumbnail directly underneath it to engage your readers.  They will easily have access to archived posts that they may normally miss out on with this free tool.

7.  **Discussion Board** - Otherwise known as a forum, community, message board, etc.  You can use this to have your readers connect with others that visit your site to share information, form connections, and help them to frequent your blog.  A forum can do wonders for your blog.  <u>Vbulletin</u> is one of the more popular message boards to use but you can find many other ones that you can embed or include on your blog.

8.  **Newsletters** - An easy way to keep track of your visitors or to build up an email list is by having a newsletter that your readers can subscribe to.  You can get one for free

through **Madmimi, iContact, Send Stream and Constant Contact** which is one of my favorites to use and even include html codes in your newsletter.

**9.  PayPal Account** - This is especially important if you plan on selling spots on your blog for others to advertise. PayPal makes it convenient for you to handle transactions securely.  Having a PayPal is also important if you want to add a donate button on your blog for your readers to contribute to.

**10.  About Me Page** - A lot of times, your readers or visitors to your blog will be curious about exactly who is sharing this information with them.  Having an about me page will give them the opportunity to get to know you, what your likes and dislikes are, and build up a bond with you that may not necessarily be accomplished without having this feature on your blog.  You can do a list of 10 Random things about you or be creative with your About me page.  After all, it is about you and will reflect your personality.  Have fun with this page!

# How to Sign up for a Google Adsense Account

Why Google Adsense?  Because Google is the granddaddy of all other pay per click advertising companies on the Internet today. There are many competitors but Google is by far the one company that you can earn a decent amount of income with every month because they work with millions of advertisers and are well known and trusted by several brands.  Due to this leverage, advertisers bid on your ad space and Google is able to offer you the highest paying ads to appear on your blog.  So, how do you sign up for a Google Adsense account?

If you are using Blogger as your platform, they make it really easy for you to do this.  When you log into your blogger dashboard, you will see a section on the left hand side where it says "earnings".  There is a video that you can watch and a step by step instructional tutorial on how you can apply to be a publisher and have your own Google Adsense account and earn some money by having advertisements run on your blog.  If you are not using Blogger as your platform, you can simply type in Google Adsense on the search engines and you can sign up for one for free using your email address.

Here are some things that you will need to have when you apply to for a Google Adsense account and what Google looks for when they are reviewing and approving publisher accounts.

- You must be at least 18 years old.
- A valid email address.
- A mailing address. Your first check will be sent in the mail.
- Your content. Make sure that you have enough content on your blog before you apply (at least 5 pages or so) before you apply for an account otherwise you may have to reapply in a couple of months again.
- Make sure your blog contains no copyrighted material meaning that you created the content yourself or you have permission by the author to post in on your blog.

Just make sure that you have enough quality content on your blog and your account will be approved and you will be able to log in daily to see how much you are earning from Google daily. Because advertisers bid and compete with each other for your advertising space, the amount that you earn will vary on a daily basis. It works on a cpc or cost per click method. Sometimes you may earn .50 a click, .75 per click, $1.00 per click and even more. So if you have a blog and you haven't signed up for a Google Adsense account, you may want to do so today and start earning money for your content.

# How to Put Ads on Your Blog

You put a lot of time and effort into your blog setting up the layout, the right template and style for you and your audience, and you are satisfied with the results.  You have even moved onto the next step by producing content for your blog on a regular basis.  So what's next?  It is time for you to incorporate ads into your blog.
How will you do this?  Where will you put them?  How can you make sure they won't be overlooked?  These questions will be answered in this article.

## How do I put Ads on my Blog?

This process is a lot easier than you may think.  Before you put any ads on your blog, you will want to sign up with a couple of companies so that you will have access to these ads.  Which companies?  You may want to try signing up for a Google Adsense account.  It may take a couple of days for your account to be approved but once it is, all you have to do is to go into the layout feature of your blog and and select the "**add a gadget**" button and scroll down until you see **Adsense** and add it.  From this point ads will automatically be displayed on your blog.  This is assuming that your adsense account has already been approved and you are using the blogger format.  If you are using Wordpress or a website, you may have to manually get the code on your Google Adsense account using a copy and paste method to place ads on your blog.  You will select a size for your advertising, highlight the html code, and then click control or CTRL button  and the letter C on your keyboard at the same time.  Next you will go to your website and select the html feature and paste them wherever you want them to be displayed.  You can paste simply by selecting the control or CTRL button on your keyboard and the letter V at the same time.

If your blog is on the Wordpress.com format, you will have to apply for a WordAds account.  This particular feature is only for allowed for bloggers with moderate to high traffic.  If you are approved as a publisher, then you will be not be allowed to run Google advertising from Google Adsense but you can use third party ads from companies like Clickbank, Payperpost, Smorty, Clickhop, Cashrocks, and others.  If you are using Wordpress.org you can download and install a wordpress plugin for your blog called WP125  for 125x125 ads to be displayed on your blog without having to manually edit your template.  This plugin will save you a lot of time.

For other third party advertising companies that you want displayed on Blogger, you will simply go to the layout of your blog, click on the "**add a gadget**" feature and scroll down until you see html/javascript and copy and paste the codes right in this section throughout your blog.  You can place them in the sidebars, under your heading, or anywhere else you see fit.

## Where should I place ads on my blog?

If you have a few ads or companies in mind that you would like to promote on your blog or website, you may be wondering where exactly they should be placed. It is recommended that they are generally above the fold, meaning they are placed above the halfway point on your page.  It is better to place them near the top of the page so that they will not be overlooked.  It is also very advisable that you place the ads near or around your content.  This is where your readers and visitors to your site will look, so you could place them there.  You can also place the ads in your content itself.  You could write a post about whatever product or products you are trying to promote and have them featured throughout your article by highlighting a certain word or phrase to with text ads instead of banner ads.  You could also do both banner advertising and text advertising.

## How to make sure my ads won't be overlooked?

This part can be somewhat tricky.  There are also a lot of factors into why you ads may be overlooked?  For example, how long are your readers staying on your blog.  If they are only there for a few short minutes, this could cause your ads to be overlooked.  The longer your readers stay on your blog, the more likely they will click on some of your ads or be enticed to do so.  How do you get your readers to stay on your blog longer?  Keep creating quality content.  You can also incorporate a free tool called Link Within that will have older related posts right underneath your current post in the form of a thumbnail where they can easily access the content.  Not only will this keep them engaged but it will bring more traffic to your blog or website over time as well.  Ultimately, the key is to try to generate some interest around what you are trying to promote by recommending it, using it yourself and writing a review on it, or any other creative ways you can think of.

## Here are a few more tips to make sure your ads aren't overlooked

After you have you mastered the technique of being able to put ads on your blog or website, it will take some adjustments and time to make sure that your ads will not be overlooked.

•I would advise that you periodically freshen up your ads and get new ones that offer specials, discounts, or promotions.
•Make sure that they are related to your content as well.  If you have a blog about cooking, Paula Deen, Martha Stewart, or Rachel Ray products may be good to promote on your site.  You will have a better click through rate, meaning your audience is more likely to click on that ad to read more about the product or service and even purchase it which will help you to earn more money.
•Try different types of ads as well.  In-line text, banner, in tag, in frame, etc.  Don't limit yourself to one type of advertising or one company to use for advertising.  This will give your audience a well-rounded selection of intriguing ads that they may respond to.

Don't get frustrated if you do not see results right away.  It took me a couple of months before I even made a whole $5 from my blog.  But I still kept blogging anyway because I loved the idea of sharing things with others.  Just keep writing good content because the reality is, the more you do this, the more traffic you will generate.  You will always be rewarded ( in more ways than one) for having targeted traffic to your blog.

# How I made $1500 in one day from Google Adsense

To be exact, the final amount was 1,494.92 less than $6 away from $1,500.  I was completely shocked, surprised and in disbelief.  I checked my account again and again and nothing changed.  I know this seems hard to believe but I have included a clip image of my Google Adsense account for proof.

**Estimated earnings**

**$25.94** ⓘ      **$1,494.92**      **$3,558.91** ⓘ
Today so far      Yesterday         This month so far

Finalized earnings may be slightly lower than estimated earnings.

You may be wondering what techniques or strategies I used in order to earn this amount?  Nothing that I know of.  The only thing that I recently did was make a Google app for one of my blogs and published it on Google Play but I have done this before and didn't notice a dramatic increase like I received yesterday.  As a matter of fact I have been quite busy this week and I just happened to check my Adsense account yesterday and noticed the staggering figure.  I wish that I did know exactly how this was achieved so that I could pass along some helpful tips to you but I have no clue as to how this happened.  I can tell you what I normally earn from Google and the most that I ever made from them in one day.

When I first started out, I was excited to earn anywhere from .50 to $1 a day.  Not a lot of money but it encouraged me to know that it really was possible to earn money from my content.  After a lot of hard work, time and considerable content that dollar turned into a few dollars and continued to go up from there.  On average, I may earn around $80 per day just on Google Adsense alone.  The most I have ever earned in one day from Google Adsense was twice the amount of my average earnings aside from what I earned yesterday.  I did notice that I had quite a lot of clicks from one of my sites which had a dramatic effect on my overall earnings.

One thing I do know is that I was completely shocked and ecstatic about and I hope to see this one day again in the future. Believe it or not, there are some bloggers or shall we say "Pro Bloggers" that no doubt frequently see this and higher amounts on a regular basis.  How do I know this?  There is a useful website called, Web of Worth that is able to estimate or calculate how much a particular blog or website is worth and how based on how much traffic and revenue is earned on a daily basis.  It is insightful and beneficial for bloggers that may be looking to either sell their blog or website or to gauge their earnings periodically to see if it is on a steady increase/decline and what can be done about it.

Do I think I will ever earn this amount again?  Anything is possible but I do not believe that I will see this amount in one day anytime in the near future.  If I do, I will certainly blog about it and hopefully have some practical tips to go along with it. Some people claim that you can't make money with Google Adsense but this post was simply to show that it is possible to earn money, even in the year 2014 with Google Adsense!

# How to Improve your Google Adsense Earnings?

Is there really a practical, reasonable way to increase your Google Adsense earnings?  If so, by how much?  If you are a blogger these are important questions to ask and have the answers to especially if you are monetizing your blog with Google Adsense.  Even if you are satisfied with your earnings, there is always room for improvement and hopefully this post will help you do just that.

I recently tried an experiment or suggestion from the many messages that I had received from Google and to my surprise it really worked.  Not only did it work but it made a big difference in my revenue.  What did I do to accomplish this? Something very simple that was worth the 6 hours that I spent making the changes.  I changed my ad units to these recommended sizes on every page on my website to 336x280, 300x250, 728x90 or 160x600.  I also made sure that I had at least 3 Adsense units on each page that had rich content. I originally had at least 104 120x600 sized unit ads and changed them to 160x600 because I was informed that the smaller ad units do not perform as well.  As I stated, it took a few hours to replace all these ad units but to my surprise it really did work.  I noticed right away that I had access to better, more visible ads than before.  It took less than 24 hours for me to notice the difference.  How much was the increase?  At least 30 percent.  That may not seem like a lot initially but most people would be estatic if they were to get at least a 30 percent raise their hourly pay.  Instead of earning $10 per hour, $13 looks a lot better. That is $120 more dollars per week, $480 per month or an extra $5,760 more per year! Well worth the time spent.

If I would have made these changes sooner, I would have reaped the benefits much earlier. Every now and then it is wise to see how your ads are performing and what you can do in a practical way to make those changes. As you can see from this experiment, it just involved a little readjustment in the size of my ads. Moving your ads up higher in the pages or placing them where your content is can also prove to be beneficial and help you to get more out of your Adsense account.

If your Google Adsense earnings seems to be on a decline lately, try to incorporate some of the methods that I utilized to see if it helps. Google will also alert you to any changes that could help your ads to perform better. It may take a little time but if it pays off in the end, it is well worth it.

# What to do if you lost your Google Adsense account?

Have you recently lost your Google Adsense account? There are a lot of people who were earning extra money from Google Adsense and have just discovered that their account was closed for no apparent reason. Has this ever happened to you? Maybe you know someone who has suffered this lost. It can be devastating, especially if your blog or website was relying solely upon Google for online income but fortunately Google is not the only company that can help bloggers earn money from home.

It is always a good idea to sign up with as many companies as you can so that you will not limit your options, earnings, and resources to one company alone. If that company decides to close down, go out of business, or in the example mentioned above sever ties with you, what will you do? Some have been forced to make the painstaking decision to forfeit their blog or website after they have put so much hard work into it. The blog that was once an asset has now become a liability to them because it is not generating enough income for the amount of time that you spend on it. Does this mean that your blog is a failure? Absolutely not. All it means is that you have to approach your blog and the goals that you have set for it with a different technique.

This is where the saying, "**Too much is never enough**" comes in. What do I mean? Let me share my own experience. When I first starting blogging I initially started with Google Adsense but I realized that there were so many other options out there for me to utilize and offer my blog readers. Had I only limited myself to this one company, I would be limiting them as well and I wanted to be able to provide access to many other resources. I figured, they would probably find them somewhere else anyway, so why not offer it on my blog. So without much hesitation, I decided to sign up with companies like Commission Junction, Share a Sale, Infolinks, Panthera Network, Roi Rocket, and a few others. Do I regret my decision? I would regret it, if I didn't do it.

You may think that signing up with several companies may snuff out your earnings from one company when in reality it will only increase your overall income in general. Don't be afraid to do this. Google is only a 1/3 of my earnings and I am glad that I choose to venture out and try some other companies to monetize my blog.

Even if you haven't lost your Google Adsense account, I would still recommend that you do this because it will not only help you to expand your reach when visitors come to your site and you can provide them with new and fresh offers keeping them on your blog longer. It will also enable you to keep your blog afloat and you can focus on creating quality content for your readers to enjoy!

With that being said, here are a few companies that you can use to monetize your blog or website.

Viglinks
Panthera Network ( highly recommend with over 200 + Partners for you to choose from)
Skimlinks
Kontera
Chickita (Very easy to get approved)
Commission Junction (Well known companies)
Share a Sale
Amazon (Commissions not very high but has tons of products here)
Linkshare
Clickbank
You could always sell your own products on using Createspace (One of my favorites)

# Top 10 Companies to Make Money from your Blog

Once you start blogging consistently, you will realize that it takes a lot of work and time to produce content. The time and effort that you put into your blog will not be in vain because you will start to see your posts being shared all over the Internet, comments are now left by your readers, and more people may even start to follow your blog. What will you do with this traffic? You could recommend services and products that would benefit them or that you use yourself by signing up with a few companies that will pay you to do this.

What kind of companies am I referring to and how does this work? You have probably heard of the term affiliate marketing if you have been on the Internet for some time. This is where businesses will reward you for each visitor or customer you bring to either try their services or use them. There are also advertising companies that will pay you simply to show and display ads along with your content on your blog. This can be done either with banner ads, in-line texts, in frame, through a blog post, and more. Some of the most common sized banner ads come with the dimension of 300 x 250 that you can put in various places throughout your blog.

Some companies will pay you by impression where an advertiser will pay you a certain amount every time an ad is displayed. Cost per click or CPC is when advertisers will pay the website owner a certain amount when the ad has actually been clicked on or through. This can also be referred to as pay per click. These are the most common methods that they use. The amount that you will get paid per click or per impression will vary daily depending upon the advertiser's budget, how much they will pay for certain keywords, the types of ads that you have on your blog and other factors. Some affiliate companies will pay you a set rate for a visitor, customer, or sign up. This rate is pretty much the same unless the advertiser makes changes but this may not happen too often.

I have a few companies that I use and have experience with to help me earn money from blogging that I think you may like to try as well. Here are my top 10 favorite companies to make money from my blog (at the moment). It is free to sign up as a publisher. Check them out today!

1. Amazon - This company is so well branded and widely known that many people that visit your site, would feel comfortable buying from them. There commission rates for affiliates are low around 4-6% per sale but I would recommend that you sign up to be a publisher because they have so many available products online.
2. Panthera Network - This is one of my all time favorites because they have so many offers and companies that they work with such as Avon, Redbox, and other well known brands. I have earned some decent money with this company.
3. Commission Junction - They have several household brands that you can use to recommend to your blog readers. Some of which include but not limited to: Sean John, Gunthy Renker, Disney, Groupon, Melissa & Doug toys, and many other companies.
4. Google Adsense - I like Google because they will place ads on your blog that will be related to your content. You will not have to pick and choose which ads would bring the best

results.  They do all of the hard work for you.

5. <u>Max Bounty</u> - This company pays some of the highest rates to publishers that I have ever seen.  The also work with brands like:  Wen hair care system, Hydrolyze, Proactive, and others.

6. <u>Infolinks</u> - They have in-line text advertising that displays in the form of lines beneath certain keywords on your blog.  This may irritate some blog readers but if you don't hear any complaints, I would definitely try this company because they are easy to sign up with.  If you don't have a lot of traffic to your blog or it is fairly new, you can still get approved for an account to make money with Infolinks.

7. <u>Share a Sale</u> - Another company that has thousands of advertisers they work with.  Whatever topic or subject your blog is based around, you can find something to promote and use on your blog at Share a Sale.

8. <u>Link Share</u> - It is somewhat similar to Commission Junction in that they have well known brands that you can sign up with like:  Hallmark, Hewlett Packard, 1800 Flowers, etc.

9. <u>Skimlinks</u> - This company allows you to earn money from their 17,000 merchants without having to wait to get approved for them to help you earn more money.  Some of the merchants have a strict approval process for publishers but Skimlinks makes this easy to overcome.

10. <u>Viglinks</u> - You can earn money from Ebay and other companies with simple links on your site.

# 25 Ways to Make Money with your Blog

Everyone knows that you can make money with your own blog or website. Most of the conventional wisdom shows that you have to do a lot of research or put all of your time into it if you really want to make a good living from it. But that's not entirely true. There are millions of bloggers that generate some extra cash simply by blogging in their spare time.

Here are just a few simple ideas to create revenue with a blog listed below:

1. Google AdSense, copy and paste some code to your blog and off you are making money.

2. Selling your ad space can be a very lucrative way of monetizing your site.

3. Affiliate marketing is another good way to make money from your blog. You join affiliate programs like CJ, ClickBank and the rest and you are paid when somebody you refer to their site makes a purchase.

4. Sponsored reviews can get you some good cash from reviewing products.

5. If you are in a niche that provides a lot of useful information to people you might consider having a 'donate' link or button.

6. You can get paid to post reviews on your blog for cash. Many refer to this as paid blogging.

7. You can promote CPA offers on your blog and make money.

8. If your blog niche discusses physical type products, you can join an affiliate program that offers physical products.

9. You can promote digital products such as eBooks and software as an affiliate.

10. In text advertisements are advertisements placed within the content on your website or blog.

11. Flip your blog to make some money on <u>Flippa</u>.

12. You can use a blog to offer a service. For example, if you are good at designing banners, you could showcase your skills and set up the blog to accept orders.

13. Offer consulting on your blog.

14. Pay Per Click (PPC) ads are usually small text links that display on your blog. When a visitor clicks the link you get a small commission.

15. Advertisers hire bloggers to write a post about their company, product, or service.

16. Sell specific products such as dog beds to specified customers; such as breeders.

17. Offer to write reviews of other people's websites.

18. Sell ad space directly to advertisers or go through an ad network.

19. Sell your services as a blogger.

20. Text Ads: These links point to the product or website, you want to advertise. When someone will click on the text ads, they will be sent to that product or website.

21. Turn your blog into a revenue site.

22. Banner Ads: In banner advertising, the advertisements will be in the form of graphics and text.

23. Products Related Advertising: In this form of advertising, you can show the ads for some particular products. You can use the products from online stores or auctions.

24. Another good way of earning from your blog is to get sponsors from different advertising agencies.

25. Amazon: Amazon is one of the top leaders for online sales. Join their affiliate program, and sell products from Amazon on your blog.

# How to Make Money with Infolinks

If you want to monetize your blog, Infolinks is a great site for bloggers to use that will reward you for your traffic. Infolinks has in line text advertising that is unique and helps to keep your content clean by not compromising it with big bold ads. They also have in search ads, in frame, and in tag ads that you can easily incorporate on your blog in less than 60 seconds. Here is more information on how Infolinks works and how you can make money with it.

Infolinks works a lot differently than traditional advertising companies because their ads are very minimal in comparison to your content. The ads are simply lines underneath certain keywords included in your content that your readers can click on and view for more information. Here is an example of in line text advertising on my other blog below. The green lines are what is called in line text advertising from Infolinks.

> $15. You can also earn more money referring your friends.
> 7. **Survey Savvy Connect** - Survey Savvy Connect is an application from Survey Savvy that will allow you to earn more money from Survey Savvy participating in surveys while you are surfing the Internet. You can download this app on your computer or mobile phone.
> 8. iPoll - iPoll used to be called Survey Head and they have so many ways for you to get paid. They will give you $5 just to sign up. You can get the cash deposited to your

Your earnings vary everyday depending upon how much money the advertisers want to spend according to their budget but you can expect to earn money every single day with Infolinks. They tend to have a higher click through rate because they are highly customizable which means additional income for you. You can check your amount daily when you log in to your publisher account online.

If you have been rejected for a Google Adsense account or have lost your account, Infolinks is a great alternative.  It is also much easier to get approved for a publisher account with Infolinks because you don't need a lot of traffic to your blog in order to get approved.  Newer blogs can also get approved through Infolinks.  Here are some frequently asked questions about Infolinks below.

## How do I sign up?

Go to Infolinks official website <u>here</u> and put in your blog details and personal information.  Make sure your email address is correct so that they can contact you regarding the status of your account and other news.

## How long does the approval process take?

It should take no longer than 3-4 business days to know whether your publisher account is approved or not. If you sign up on a Friday, you will have to factor in Saturday and Sunday and not count these as business days.  You may not hear anything back until the following Wednesday or even Thursday.

## When do I get paid?

You will get paid 45 days after the end of the month when your account reaches the payment threshold.  Payment thresholds can be set at $50 or $100.  You can pick which one is more convenient for you.

## What methods of pay do they offer?

They have a variety of payment methods.  You can choose Paypal, Bank Wire, eCheck, Western Union, Payoneer, or ACH.

## How do I put Infolinks on my blog?

You can copy and paste the script in the html code page of your site manually.  For Blogger, Joomla, Wordpress, and Drupal there is a plugin that will easily integrate the ads for you automatically.  You just pick which blog you use and it completes this step for you.  So easy!

## How much will I earn?

It is hard to say but my earnings have gradually increased with Infolinks since I started using them a few months ago. Here are some of my payment proofs from the last 3 months from Infolinks.

| Month | Description | Earnings | Total |
|---|---|---|---|
| March 2013 | Earnings for this month (3/1/2013 - 3/31/2013) | $44.78 | |
| | **Total earnings for March** | | **$44.78** |
| April 2013 | Earnings carried from previous month | $44.78 | |
| | Earnings for this month (4/1/2013 - 4/30/2013) | $36.86 | |
| | **Total earnings for April** | | **$81.64** |
| | Payment issued on June 1, 2013 | | $81.64 |
| May 2013 | Earnings for this month (5/1/2013 - 5/31/2013) | $48.75 | |
| | **Total earnings for May** | | **$48.75** |

I only have Infolinks on one of my blogs and not on my main website. If I did, I would probably earn more.

If you are thinking about other ways to make money from your blog, give Infolinks a try.

# How you can Make Money with Panthera Network

Recently, I posted a payment proof from <u>Panthera Network</u> on my other blog at <u>Homebased Mommie</u> for a little over $700 in one month. You can go there and read the post and see the payment proof from Panthera and some other companies that paid me as well. If you have a blog or website or plan to, you can definitely use this company to earn some decent income from home and I will show you how to do this.

First of all you may be wondering, what is <u>Panthera Network</u>? It is a fortune 500 company that has around 300 active promotions, offers, and products that you can recommend to others and earn money while doing so. They work with well known trusted brands like Amazon, Netflix, Avon, Redbox, Fiverr, Expedia, GSN, Fandago, and so many more. It is the best affiliate marketing company, in my opinion on the Internet today! They have the highest payouts, excellent customer support, and will even reveal your stats to you in real time. If you refer someone to join a program or company, you will see your referral earnings immediately on your dashboard. I have had more success with this affiliate company than any other affiliate company to date. My personal affiliate manager even called me via telephone to help me with promotions, tracking, and any other questions I had.

After my account was approved, to my surprise, I was even sent a gift card from Starbucks in the mail just for signing up and I hadn't even made any money yet.

If you have a blog or website and would like to earn passive income, please check out **Panthera Network**. Here is what you need to know to get started with Panthera Network as a publisher.

1.  Go to their official website **here** and sign up to be a publisher.
2.  Put in all your personal information, including your blog, blog stats, email address, etc.
3.  Wait for about business 3 days to find out the status of your publisher account.

After you are approved, you can start promoting several companies on your blog in the form of banner ads, text, email marketing, etc. No matter what your blog topic is centered around, you can find something on Panthera Network to recommend to your blog readers. Your commissions will add up quickly, especially if you have a large following or frequent visitors to your blog or site.

Panthera Network also has bonuses for new publishers that give for the first 60 days. They are as follows:
•$150 reward cash bonus if you generate $1,500 in commissions for the first 60 days
•$1,000 bonus check for Super Affiliates if you generate $25,000 in commissions in the first 60 days

In addition to this, you can also earn points for every dollar you earn on Panthera Network. If you earn $1 in commission sales, you will have 10 points. These points can be used for cash rewards or gift cards. It is just another way to earn even more money from Panthera Network.

If you haven't had much success with some of the other affiliate companies, I would definitely recommend that you give Panthera Network a try and sign up today! If for some reason, your publisher account is not approved, please contact them via phone or email and they may approve your account the following day. If not, they will tell you exactly what you need to do so that you can reapply again.

# How to Make Money with Job Boards

**There are so many ways to earn money with your very own blog or website. One unique way to do this is with job boards. What do I mean by this? Many of you have probably heard of sites like Monster, Indeed, and Career Builder. They list the most current companies hiring at the moment. You can use sites like these to make extra money just by placing them on your page. I will show you how to do this.**

You may be wondering what the benefit could possibly be of doing this and I have two good reasons. First, it is free content for your site. This does not let you off the hook for creating content yourself but it will give your visitors more content to read over. It can also keep your readers coming back because the job leads are updated regularly. It is also an easy way to earn passive income from these job sites.

**Just a side note: If your is blog not geared towards employment, careers, job seekers, income revenue, or anything related to this topic it may not be as effective. You will always want to consider your blog readers interests before you introduce or feature a certain theme or subject to them.**

So, how exactly would you go about featuring this on your site and what do you need to get started?  All you need is a place to put your job leads on.  You can feature a widget or snippet of it on your homepage or even add a page and devote it entirely to job listings.  Many sites will also allow you to choose from RSS feeds, text links, banners, logos, search boxes, and job boxes.  It is really up to you to decide exactly where you will feature them on your blog but I find it more beneficial to place them on the more prominent or visible places on your blog.

It is much easier than you may think to get started featuring jobs on your blog or website.  Here are the steps.

1.  Type in Job Boards or something similar to this on Google and it will bring up a list of companies that advertise current jobs.
2.  Pick from the available sites listed and check out what kind of jobs they feature.
3.  Scroll down to the bottom of their homepage and look for affiliate, affiliate program, or API, etc.
4.  Sign up for free to be a publisher.  You may be required to give them your blog stats including how many visitors you reach per day, week, month, etc, the age of your blog, category, and so forth.
5.  After your publisher account has been approved, you will be allowed to embed them on your blog with a simple html code that you can copy and paste wherever you like.

It is really that simple.  Now you are finished you can log into your account every day to see how much you have earned.  Each time a visitor to your site clicks on job or potential job to view, you will earn extra revenue.

Where does this revenue come from?  You will get a percentage of what the advertisers pay these job sites to list them on your blog. You are somewhat of a third-party beneficiary of their advertising budget. If you like the idea of being able to offer free, useful content to your readers and be able to earn some extra money from your blog, you may want to try using job boards to accomplish this. Here are some sites that will pay you to do this.

Monster - You will have to go through Commission Junction to sign up to be a publisher.
Indeed - Go to their official website and sign up for free by selecting API
Careerjet - You can sign up on their official website here become a Careerjet affiliate
Career Builder - You will need to send them an email and wait for your account to be approved.
Simply Hired - Another site that is easy to sign up with.

I would also recommend that you use well-known or the more popular job boards to make sure they feature reputable employers. Here is a snippet of some of my publisher earnings from Indeed below.

| 2013-07-01 | Balance forward | | $192.98 |
| 2013-07-31 | Earnings - referrals | $30.32 | |
| | Balance due to publisher | | $223.30 |

Check out some of the companies and sign up to be a publisher today!

# Top 5 Effective Ideas to Monetize your Blog

Blogs are not only making money for millions of bloggers from all across the globe but also helping over a million of bloggers to earn a salary.  According to an article published on Social Media Today website, about 14% of bloggers are earning a salary through blogging, which simply indicates how profitable a blog can be if rightly built up and monetized.  There are many effective blog monetization techniques.  The following are the top 5 ideas to take your blog from a hobby to profit:

## 1.  Selling Your Own Product or Service

Having your own product or service is one of the best ways to make money on the Internet. Unlike selling others products or services you keep 100 percent of the profits selling your own product or service through your blog.  Information products can be profitable for you because there is little or no overhead associated with marketing and selling those products.

## 2.  Affiliate Marketing

Affiliate marketing is when you promote someone else's products or services resulting in a sale or any other specific action performed by your referrals, and earn a commission or flat fee for it.

If done right, it can be a very profitable business with your blog. You can become an affiliate for your blog's web hosting provider, for example. If someone goes to your web hosting company's website through the affiliate link given to you by the webs hosting company and purchases a hosting service, then you will earn a commission or flat fee for the sale. There is an endless list of products and services you can choose from to get started with this program. Choose several reputable programs that are related to your blog's niche.

## 3. Membership Blog Sites

This is a wonderful blog monetization technique which gives your blog members access to a private membership area on your blog for a fixed and ongoing monthly membership fee. In this membership area, you would give privilege to members who agree to pay you a monthly fee for accessing valuable and very useful content such as special blog posts, reports, video tutorials, eBooks, etc. This is a nice passive income business model which can provide you with a regular and steady monthly income.

## 4. Sell Private Advertising Space

You can sell space on your blog to advertisers who would want to put up their advertising block on your blog. You can sell more than one space. If you have eight spaces and sell each space for $50, then you will make $400 from eight spaces. You really need to build up the traffic to use this blog monetization method. However, some people do not like ads on their blog. It is really a personal preference.

## 5. Run Online Ads

This is one of the most widely use methods by bloggers from around the world.  If you have a blog with a sizeable amount of traffic, then running various online ads can be a source of substantial income with your blog.

Google AdSense is the most popular online ad program you can use to monetize your blog.  There are various types of Google AdSense ads such as PPC (Pay Per Click) and CPM (Cost Per Mile or Thousand).  The most popular online ad is the PPC ad which enables you to earn money when any visitor to your blog clicks on an advertisement placed on the web pages of your blog.  Since Google strategically places related ads on your blog, the chance of getting more clicks on the ads are high.

**Final Words**

You can earn decent money through blogging.  Remember, content is the king.  If you want to make money with your blog, the most important thing to do is to write informative and unique content for your audience.  Always write useful and interesting posts and then publish them on your blog on a regular basis.  If you write two or three posts a week, make sure you keep up with the schedule.  Finally, start with one method and then add on others to build multiple streams of income.

# How to Make a Video Game Website

Have you ever played video games online or dreamed of having your own video gaming website?  You may not realize it but a video gaming site is one of the easiest ways to start your own blog especially if you find it challenging to come up with a topic or subject that you would like to blog on.  I will show you how I did this and how you can too, using <u>MyArcade Plugin Pro</u> and some other tools.

In order to start your own fully functional arcade website you will need to purchase hosting with sufficient bandwith so that your site will be capable of handling multiple players and visitors to your site at a time.  You can try sites like <u>Go Daddy</u>, <u>Host Gator</u>, <u>Blue Host</u>, and any others that you prefer.  Make sure that your hosting comes with Wordpress so that it will be easy for you to install your plugin.  If you are not sure how much bandwith you will need, you could select the unlimited bandwith option or talk to your hosting provider regarding the My Arcade Plugin Pro that you would like to install and they will assist you with this.

You will need a domain name as well for your site.  Sometimes you can get a discount or even a free domain with a hosting plan for at least the first year or for little as just 99 cents.  If you can't think of a unique name, your hosting provider might even think of a creative one for you.  They did this for me because all the ones that I thought of had already been taken.

After you have your hosting and domain name you will need to install Wordpress.  This step is very simple also and will only take you a few minutes to complete with just a few clicks with your mouse.

When this step is completed, you will need to log into your Wordpress account and start enabling some plugins.  You could use the free My Arcade Plugin and search for it on Wordpress and it will install it for you.  It comes with a free theme and everything you need to have a professional looking arcade site.  If you want even more features the My Arcade Plugin Pro will meet and even exceed your goals.  It will cost you $30 to purchase this software and is well worth it because it will allow you to automatically fetch games from over 10 gaming distributors and allow you to manually import games on your site also.  It comes with a Fun Games theme to enhance and customize your games.  This theme and plugin is Wordpress ready and will post and fetch new games every day for your users to play online!  If you are already familiar with Wordpress you could complete your site in just a few minutes.

Because My Arcade Plugin Pro is a plugin that you will have to purchase, you will have to download it to your computer and upload it to your server or hosting provider.  They give you step by step instructions when you purchase the product.  You can also go to the My Arcade Plugin Pro official website and select the support feature and there is a short list of steps that you will have to follow.  After that final step has been completed, all you have to do is fetch your games to get it started, customize and manage them, enable even more free plugins (if you like) and you are ready to go!

Anybody can have an arcade website without any coding knowledge or experience whatsoever.  Because the games are automatically fetched and published for you all you have to do is to go into your Wordpress account and delete the games you do not want featured and displayed on your site, which only takes seconds to do.

You can even earn money with your very own arcade website because you can sign up to be a publisher for companies like Mochi Media and Big Fish Games

and earn money per impression, each time a game is played, and so forth.  Make sure that you upload your special publisher key code which is a group of numbers and possibly a combination of letters to your server or hosting provider so they can verify your blog or website.  If you fail to complete this step, you will not get credit for the games being played on your site if you have signed up to be a Mochi Media publisher.

You may be wondering how much all of this will cost you.  You can get hosting from $1.99 per month up to $7 per month that may come with your own domain. If not, a domain name can cost you around $10 per year.  The My Arcade Plugin Pro is a one time $30 fee, unless you choose to use the free My Arcade Plugin and not go with the pro version.

If you want to build a fun, entertaining website in a very short time and have your visitors come back to play new games, use the My Arcade Plugin pro script to help your vision come to life. You can check out my video gaming site here and also read more about My Arcade Plugin pro and more of its unique features online.

# 7 Tips on How you can Boost Traffic

**The Internet is a wonderful thing. Through the power of the World Wide Web, you can express yourself creatively, give voice to your opinions, share your experiences with the world and even make money or help your business grow.**

However, whether you have a website for personal or professional purposes, it seems like a very wasteful use of space if not very many people drop by your site. For whatever purpose your website serves, anything that's put on the Internet is meant to be seen and seen by many people. It's the only way to maximize the Internet as a resource. Here are seven helpful tips that might help you boost your website's traffic.

## Provide Great Content

First and foremost, if people are going to go to your site then you better have something worth coming back to. Your content, regardless of what type of content you specialize in has to be up to par and be able to compete with what other sites with similar content about similar topics can offer. Great content not only ensures that a visitor of your site comes back for more but a person that is happy with your site would most likely share and promote your site, leading to more visitors.

## Use Keywords and Learn Other SEO Basics

If you have a blog or website and have never heard of search engine optimization (SEO), now would be the perfect time to read up on it.  SEO is a practice content providers do in order for sites or specific webpages to get featured more prominently on search engines thereby drumming up more traffic.  (People who go on search engines usually only search up to the second or third page of the search results.)  Learn how to use keywords (terms that people tend to type in search engines) and to integrate them properly into your content.

## Link Trading

Working with other sites that provide similar content to your and have them link your site from theirs and vice versa is a great method of increasing traffic.  Readers interested in something would always prefer to read more about it.  They see your site amount the links provided by a website they trust or like regularly visit and they'll most likely pay your site a visit too.  This not only generates more traffic but also allows you to form positive professional relationships with other sites.

## Social Media

Sites like Facebook, Twitter, Google Plus and others exist for a reason far more important than posting selfies.  These social networking sites are a great way to promote your site.  Use your friends, the friends of your friends-and their friends as well-to get your traffic up.

**Advertise**

If you have the money, why not use some of it to advertise, especially if your website is a key tool in your business? Pay per click is the ideal way to go. Just be sure you advertise in the right websites, like how financial sites usually have ads in financial comparison sites or toy stores advertise in geek related websites. Know your market and you can gauge which sites to place your ad in.

**Dress Up Your Website**

This may seem like a small, superficial thing but a good looking website (that's still efficient) tends to attract visitors. Again, it depends on the type of website you have but essentially, dazzling your audience with pics and videos and a hot layout is a great way to keep your readers from bouncing to other sites instead.

**Free Stuff**

Must like with advertising, if you can fund giving away free stuff from time to time, do it. This will definitely generate a lot of traffic for your site as everyone likes getting free stuff. A lot of the sites do it and it is always effective. Movie review sites give away DVD'S, comparison sites sometimes provide the occasional free service and other sites provide coupons. These are little things that are going to make your readers consistently flock back to your website.

# 5 Ways to Get Free Steady Traffic to your Blog

Most people will tell you that starting your own blog can be a challenge but getting steady traffic to your blog can be one of the hardest things to overcome. Before you give up too easily, remember this one tip. Go where the people are. The question is, where are they? The simple most obvious answer is online but exactly where are they online and how can you navigate or direct them to your blog is what will be discussed in this post today.

No doubt, you will come to realize that not everyone will appreciate your blog. For example, if you have 1,000 visitors to your blog in one day but they only stay on your site for under a minute, chances are they may have been looking for something else. You want to reach those who have an interest in your blog's topics and discussions. Lets say you have a coupon blog, trying to gain an audience from people who are interested in Internet marketing may not be the best strategy. You will not garner the attention and traffic that your blog deserves not because it is unworthy but because you have not reached your targeted audience. On the other hand, if you visit and frequent sites and places where people are looking to save money on a coupon forum community or discussion board the outcome of my example would be totally different. Instead of 1,000 visitors per day for just a few seconds, now you have 200 visitors and they stay on your blog for an hour or so is a much better scenario for you and your blog.

This doesn't have to be a pain-staking process or consume a lot of your time.  There are some avenues or routes that you can pursue to direct readers to your blog who are searching for the very things you talk about.  Here are some suggestions that will help you to effectively get free, steady traffic to your blog.

**1.**  YouTube - It is the second largest search engine in the world and not to be underestimated.  There are millions of people searching YouTube for various things online and you can use this to your advantage.  Start a channel surrounding your blog topics and even highlight some beneficial tips and information in your videos to direct people to your blog.  If they like what you share, they will want to find out more and your blog is the perfect solution.  It is recommended that you vlog or make videos on a regular basis to grow your channel and to keep your audience interested.

**2.**  Apps - Almost everyone is using a smartphone these days and if your site has mobile capabilities, you can get an app for your blog or website.  You can either choose to get an iphone app for $100 or one on Google play for a one time price of $25 or both.  This cost is minimal in comparison to the steady flow of traffic that you will get just having an app for your site.  It is convenient, easily accessible, and gives your readers more options to get the information they need.

3.  Ebook - An ebook is a very effective way to get your blog noticed.  If this is the first time you will publish an ebook for your site just remember that because you are a new author and introducing yourself to the public (so to speak), it may take a few months for it to build momentum.  This is especially true if you do not promote your ebook at all.  You will find in just a few short months, people will buy your book and read it.  It will stay there on Amazon or wherever

you decide to publish it forever so it will be a steady stream of traffic to your blog or website.  You can even publish your book for free through Createspace, an Amazon company in as little as 5 days. **Side Note:**  The album Thriller by Michael Jackson took over a year to become a best-seller.

4. Forum - Have a community embed in your blog or website is always a great way to get steady traffic.  Some visitors may frequent your site just for that support and family environment that you can find in an online community.  Incorporating a discussion board is a great way to get steady traffic to your blog.

5. Q & A Community - If you notice most Google searches are in the form of a question.  You have probably searched for something yourself in the form of a question as well.  With a question and answer site, you will be able to reach those who may not have necessarily found your blog just by incorporating this feature.  It is also great for SEO purposes.  Your site will also be looked at as a go-to- type of site to find answers to questions that are centered around your blog topics or interests.

These are just a few ways that you can use to get free steady traffic to your blog or website.  If you are struggling with this issue, why not try some or all of these methods today.  Don't be afraid because you have never tried them before thinking that you will fail.  Remember your audience is out there, you are simply using these methods to go where the people are.

# How to Make Your Blog Stand Out

**Making your blog stand out can be compared to a model trying to get a modeling contract or a singer trying to get a recording contract. You know that there are other models and singers that can sing or look just as good or even better than you. Is there something or anything that you can do to get noticed? For a blogger this can be particularly challenging but not impossible and this post will explain exactly how you can do this.**

Let's say you have a Coupon blog and you start to notice that there are hundreds and thousands of other coupon blogs. How will you make your blog stand out from the others? Some may say that this is easier said than done but there are some easy ways that you can make your blog shine and illuminate above your competition. Here are 10 different things you can try to accomplish this.

**1.** Come up with a catchy or memorable name for your blog. Something that will stick in your reader's head. Musicians are really good at doing this when coming up with a name for their album or song. Here are some examples: Funky Cold Medina by Tone Loc, Bootlylicious by Beyonce, Scream & Shout by Britney Spears and Will.i.Am. Instead of naming your coupon blog Deals & Steals you could try these titles Coupon Diva Queen, Krazy for Coupons, or Coupon Junkie.

**2.** Primp your blog the same as you would if you were to redesign or redecorate your home, a wardrobe, your car, etc. Use a mixture of colors for your blog design or those that are bright or reflective of your personal style. Use beautiful images or glittery graphics. Play around with the fonts and templates to make it stand out and look more professional.

**3.** Show your personality throughout your posts. This could even been done when explaining how to do something. If you are naturally funny or witty, include this when you write. Write exactly how you would speak if you were talking to someone in person. For example, when talking about the smokey eye effect you could say, "When you have achieved the perfect smokey eye look, not only will it give your eyes drama but everyone in the room will drop their jaws and stare in amazement wanting to know who's that girl.

**4.** Interact with your readers. Make time for them. No one likes to visit or frequent a blog where the blogger seems invisible. By that I mean, if someone leaves a comment make sure you acknowledge it or respond. If they send you an email reply, get back in touch with them as soon as possible. Ask questions in your post about any related experiences they can share or contribute. This will keep them connected with you.

**5.** Add a community. A forum or online discussion board is a great way to make your blog stand out. They may even visit your blog more frequently just to see what the members are talking about and even start contributing themselves.

**6.** Give them visuals. Lets say you are writing a post about how to achieve a certain hairstyle or look, could you include a photo or series of photos showing your before and after look. You could also make a video tutorial showing how to do this as well. This will add more value to your posts and make your blog have more credibility.

**7.** Giveaways and freebies. Almost everyone likes freebies and so you could offer some free items for your readers and promote a giveaway from time to time. Make sure that it is related to your blog theme or something that they would be interested in having or purchasing for themselves. Contests are also a great way to get your readers involved and can give your blog some steam or a much needed boost.

**8.** Check out your competition, preferably those who blogs tend to stand out, are frequently visited, and generate a lot of comments to see what you could do to improve your own blog. You don't need to copy their style but you can for example, talk about something they don't or haven't talked about or offer a service or feature that will appeal to your audience.

**9.** Be creative with your posts. All of us probably have many ideas running in our heads and you can use your blog to get those ideas out. This will prove to be especially effective if they are in harmony with your blog theme.

**10.** Keep it fresh. Do not forget to keep producing great content on a regular basis. Some of the best blogs can lose their audience if they fail to give their readers something new and fresh to read.

These are just some basic tips that will help to make your blog stand out. Try to utilize as many of these into your blog as you can and check your results. Before you know it, your blog will be the **one** to follow and will definitely stand out.

# 5 Easy Ways to Promote Your Blog

Traffic to a blog is like customers to a store or patrons to a restaurant.  No matter how good the food is, without customers it may quickly go out of business.  The same is true in a relative sense in regards to your blog.  You will need traffic, if your intention is to have a second income or to work from home full time as a blogger.

This is where promotion will come into play.  There are numerous ways for you to be able to do this.  From paid advertising, link exchanges, to article submission and so much more.  Patience is also needed as well, especially if your blog is brand new.  It will take time for you to reach your audience but when you do, you will want to keep your audience engaged by writing quality content regularly according to your own schedule. Here are some easy ways to promote your blog or website that I have used and implicated myself that have proved to be very effective.

1.  **YouTube** - There are plenty of video submission sites but YouTube has given me the most results and promotion for my blogs and that is why I included it first. Some fun facts about YouTube is so vital in promoting your blog.  YouTube gets over 1 Billion unique visitors to their site every month and according to Nielsen, they are able to reach more adults 18-34 than any cable network.  These stats alone validate why someone would want to start their very own YouTube channel to promote their site and get directly in front of their audience.

2. **Writing an Ebook** - This is an excellent way to promote your blog for life! Literally.  **<u>Createspace</u>** is a great free tool that will

design, arrange, set up, and publish your ebook to sell on Amazon, **Createspace's** stores, and many other worldwide channels.  You can put a link to your blog in your ebook and promote your site to every reader and buyer of your book and earn money for the sales of your book in the process.  This is another guaranteed way to promote your blog with no cost to you.

**3.  Social Media** - Use Facebook, Twitter, Instagram, Linkedin, Pinterest, Stumble Upon, Reddit, and other social media networks to your advantage and promote your blog.  You want to use this at your discretion because your main purpose for social media is to connect with your followers and build up a relationship with them.  If your blog has valuable content, they will automatically do this for you.  They will share your blog, articles, posts, etc. with their friends, family, and others.  If you constantly promote your blog or try to sell them things all the time, your audience may get turned off.

**4.  Fiverr** - Use Fiverr to promote your blog.  There are so many ways for you to do this on Fiverr through video testimonials, radio advertising, graphics and images, and more!  The best part is that it only costs $5 and sometimes a little more if you want add ons.

5. **Business Cards/Flyers** - This is the traditional way of promoting your blog but can prove to be very effective as well.  You can put up flyers just about anywhere in your neighborhood, on grocery store bulletin boards, distribute in random places while you are traveling and anywhere else that you can think of or any area that gets a lot of traffic.  If you have a work at home blog, you could leave your business cards in the unemployment office or at other government offices.

I am sure you can think of so many more but I just listed a few that I have tried and have worked for me.  What are your favorite ways to promote your blog?

# How Long will it take to Make Money Blogging?

In the beginning of my blogging journey, I had asked myself this question several times over in my mind. Maybe you have too. It can next to impossible to put a time frame on exactly when you will make money because there are quite a few factors involved. Some of which include: If you are monetizing your blog and what methods you are using to do so, how much traffic you receive to your blog, and how much you plan to earn from blogging in general. If you have decided to monetize your blog, I can assure you that you will earn some money so don't give up too soon. I will share with you my own personal experience and how long it actually took me to start making money blogging.

A couple of years ago, I decided to start my very own blog. I had absolutely no idea what I was doing, how to design a blog, how often to blog, and so on. I was determined to give it a try because I had already been writing for companies like Hubpages, Squidoo, and Textbroker, so why not for my own blog. It was the best decision I ever made creatively and financially. But I had a long road ahead of me. Let me explain.

Being a rookie blogger was terrifying to me. I knew the formula for blogging because of my previous experience writing online. But would this guarantee that I could earn money with my own blog? Not necessarily. I always adopted the idea, that you will never know how something will turn out unless you try. And that is exactly what I did and have been doing for the past 2 years. So, how much did I make?

In my very first month of blogging I earned a whopping $1.93. Not very impressive, but it did give me some hope that this could be accomplished. The next month I doubled my earnings. It took me six months to reach the $100 mark. At the time, I was only relying upon one company to monetize my blog and that was a **big** mistake. It is much better to spread your wings, so to speak, and utilize as many streams of revenue for yourself as possible. Especially if they are related to your blog or audience. Even though I was only earning a few dollars initially, it did convince me that you really can make money blogging.

I decided to come up with a strategy. I figured if I could earn $100, I could earn $200. What did I do? I came up with a game plan. I would pursue blogging very aggressively treating like it was my own business. Here are some things I did to accomplish this in no particular order.

1. **Blogged at the least 3 times a week.**
2. **Had a presence on social media.**
3. **I connected with others in my niche.**
4. **Checked out my competition.**
5. **Tried different things (Q & A page on my site)**
6. **Eventually got a YouTube channel.**
7. **Talked about things that I would be interested in myself.**
8. **Answered questions from others that were related to my blog.**

As you can see, there was no magic formula and not too difficult to do. Did it work? A year and a half later, my earnings quadrupled. Two years later, I earn a full time living blogging online but it didn't happen overnight. It took a lot of hard work, time, patience, effort, persistence, determination, humility, and the list goes on and on. I tried not to take myself too seriously when I got on YouTube because you will subject yourself to a lot of criticism but you will also get positive feedback as well. I do not regret the decision because YouTube has really jump started my overall online revenue. Without it, I am not sure if I would be earning a full time living blogging yet.

So what about you,when will you make money blogging? If you already have a large following on social media, there is a great possibility that you can earn money blogging faster than if you were just starting from scratch. I can't say exactly when that will be but if you continue to focus on your content, have a passion for your subject, really connect with your readers, and take your blog just as serious as if you had your very own business, you will make money blogging.

# 8 Ways to Deal with Writer's Block

**Writers-even the best ones, the cream of the crop, the wittiest, most charming writers of all time- have, at one time or another, experienced the dreaded attack of 'writer's block.'**

This is what happens when writers are faced with a blank page and find themselves unable to write even a single sentence, phrase or word.  They may spend hours or days looking at the vast, emptiness of that white page or blank screen and announce, in the direst tones, "I have writer's block."

This can last from days to weeks to years.  In some cases, writer's block has forced many to abandon a project, a new book or even a career in writing.  For those who persevere though, the rewards could turn out sweet.  So, if you get writer's block, don't be discouraged right away.  Here are some tips you could follow to get you back on writing's good graces:

**Do something else.**  Pour your creative juices onto something else like painting, designing, scrap booking or even re-decorating your room.  Work on that for hours or days and then go back to your writing.

Sometimes, writing the whole time may decrease your

productivity and creativity. Learn to jump from one art to another to shake your creative juices loose.

**Do free writing.** Sometimes, it helps when you just write whatever is in your mind. Spend some minutes in your day to just write freely, ignore punctuation and grammar and allow it to be totally random. Always carry a notebook with you. Ricky Lee once said in a university seminar that he had tons of unpublished manuscripts set aside because sometimes, he really just liked to write-not because he needed to meet a deadline or finish a project. He wrote just for the sake of writing. And that spontaneity, that impulsiveness, has made him love it more.

**Start whenever you please.** Don't worry if you start in 'medias res' or in the middle part of a story. Chronology isn't as important in the beginning. You could start with the ending and just work your way to the beginning of the story or article or essay. Edgar Allan Poe, one of the most famous writers of all time, started some of his stories writing the ending first.

**Move.** It doesn't help your mind and body if you only sit in front of your computer for hours on end. If there's nothing happening to your screen or paper, if there's no movement there, then move. Dance, learn yoga, go to the mall or swim. Exercise is also good. Movement helps because it improves circulation and circulation means more oxygen and blood to the brain, which means improved higher brain functions-which, basically means, you'll have more energy to write.

**Meditate.** A relaxed mind help you be more imaginative.

Though some folks can write with rock music blasting through the background, plenty of old-school writers still prefer solitude or at least a writing environment with less distractions. This way, they're able to focus more and write better.

**Stay away from distractions.** If the distractions really prove insurmountable, do something to get rid of them. Either turn off your phone or disconnect from the Internet. Clean your workspace. If you happen to work beside people who like to play their music loud, or if the construction work in the next room, and the noise is really bothering with you, then it would be better if you get yourself a new set of headphones with noise-cancelling features.

**Spend some time away from writing.** Do something else. Shop. Have fun with friends. Cook a meal you've never cooked before. Go on a trip. Some people release some of their stress this way. However, just remember not to go past your spending. Writers aren't exactly known for being smart with money. For most writers, money is a nice incentive but it doesn't make the world go round. So they spend their money on books instead of food, or shoes or clothes they need. Don't be a cliche'. Maxing out your **savings** or **credit card** might make you feel good today-especially if the writing isn't going so well-but it'll leave you with more problems in the long run. So when you try to escape writing blues, spend only as much as you could afford to lose-and no more than that.

**Write as you wake up.** Write when you're still half asleep. Put a notepad by the bed and the moment you open your eyes, write the first few things that come to your mind. You'll have fun discovering what you think of when you're only half lucid.

Apply these tips, and hopefully, you'll find that managing and overcoming writer's block is easy-with the right motivation and attitude.

# 8 Tips to Keep you Motivated when starting your own Blog or Website

As I am writing this article, I will be applying some of the tips to myself because there will be days when you lack motivation, especially when you are just starting out with your own blog or website. At times you may feel good and be very enthusiastic about your blog. Then there are times when doubts arise or you feel overwhelmed. You may even question whether it is really worth it or not. It is normal part of the process when you are starting your own business because the truth is your blog is your business. Anytime you take a risk a little bit of anxiety or even fear will arise from time to time. But if you give up now, how will you ever know what the outcome will be? Of course the answer is that you won't know. No worries. Here are some practical tips that you can apply right now to keep you motivated when starting your own blog or website.

**1. Be Realistic -** Rome wasn't built in a day and the same can also apply to a successful blog or website. It takes time. Just think of some successful companies or blogs. Subway, Google, Twitter, and even Papa John's wasn't a household name a few years ago. It takes time. Time to build a following, a name for yourself, and loyal readers. And if you stick with it, they will be loyal to the end.

**2. Reflect -** This is very important to do from time to time because sometimes you may tend to focus on what you haven't achieved instead of what you have. Look back and see how far you have come. Try this exercise: Check your stats from a year ago. Have they improved? Maybe initially, you only had a few visits per week but now you have hundreds. What were you earning 6 months or even a year ago? Maybe you started out only making a few cents a day but now it you are earning a few dollars or even more. Do you have more people returning to your site? More Facebook likes? If you try this exercise, you will be encouraged and may come to find out that you are doing better than you originally thought.

**3. High Expectations -** Try to avoid having too many high expectations in the beginning. Take baby steps. You have to walk before you can run. It is practical to have goals for your blog or website but you also want to make sure that they are reachable because if not, you could set yourself up for disappointment.

**4. Avoid Comparison -** Try not to compare yourself with others. Sometimes this is really hard to do but remember that everybody's circumstance is different. It would be unrealistic to expect the same outcome for yourself that others may have had. Although it is beneficial to check out your competition periodically, try to avoid comparing your site with theirs. People appreciate different sites for different reasons. Remember that your blog or site is unique and like no one else's.

**5. Get Feedback -** Talk to a very close friend or your spouse or partner. Someone that knows you well and has your best interest at heart. I have done this many times and I have never regretted doing so. They will give you encouragement and be supportive of you and your endeavors. We all need encouragement on occasion and that is what a good friend or spouse is built for. They may even offer suggestions and advice on ways you can improve.

**6. Color -** Why would this be a factor for motivation, you may wonder? Because color can have an affect on our mood, the way the we work, and even function. Color can also be very inspiring. Even when you are having a bad day and the sun is shining bright, somehow it seems to put you in a better mood. That is because the color yellow exudes happiness. Purple has a calming effect, and orange can inspire you. If you can't paint your home office you can use color to motivate you in other ways. Here are a few ideas to incorporate color into your work space:

**Candles**
**Pillows**
**Throws**
**Mousepad**
**Pens**
**Colored paper**
**Rugs**
**Plants**
**Chair**

**7. Look for blogs that inspire you -** Find a blogs or websites that is in your area of expertise or niche that you get inspiration from.  Read their background story of how they got started and obstacles they had to overcome.  Many of them started out with the same hurdles that you may be facing but never gave up and that will encourage you to continue.  Try to avoid comparing or copying another website.

**8.  Dream -** It is good to envision what you want to achieve from your blog or website.  It can motivate you in so many different ways.  It can also help you to set practical goals for yourself without feeling overwhelmed.  Write them down on paper.  Who knows, in a few months you may have reached or even surpassed your goals.  You are more likely to reach your goals if you set them.

# Final Thoughts on Starting a Blog

If you are having second thoughts about starting your own blog, put them out of your mind? I did the same thing myself. When back and forth on the idea of starting my own blog wondering if I can really do this, am I capable enough of doing so, will it really work and so many other questions? I think it is natural to have some anxiety and worries because you want your blog to be successful. Don't let your fears keep you from trying something new.

In hindsight, I wish that I would have started my blog(s) much sooner because I learned a lot about starting my own business, I have been able to come in contact with people that I may not have reached without my blog and it has also helped me to earn steady income from home.

If you have tried everything else that you could possibly think of online, why not give blogging a try? If you apply some of the tips and techniques that are contained within this book, your blog is sure to make an impact on the web. You will be proud of yourself and have a visual presence online to show for it.

I know you can do this. Why not get started today and come up with a plan to give it your all for at least 6 months. Longer if you are able to do so. Create quality content on a regular basis, share your content online, monetize it and continue to promote it. Everybody is waiting for the next big thing and it just may be your blog or website.

If you are seriously thinking about starting your own blog or website today, make sure you go to: <u>Go Daddy</u> (to acquire a blog) Blogger or <u>Weebly</u> (free blog).  You can also get hosting from <u>Blue Host</u>, <u>Host Gator</u>(hosting) and many others.  I wish you the best with your blogs!!!

www.ingramcontent.com/pod-product-compliance
Lightning Source LLC
Chambersburg PA
CBHW060453060326
40689CB00020B/4517